I0041168

30 DAY RESET:
Brand, Business
& Bottom Line

True stories from entrepreneurs

By Karen Taylor Bass

TAYLORMADE BOOKS

US $16.95
CANADA $19.95

30 DAY RESET:
Brand, Business
& Bottom Line
True stories
from entrepreneurs

By Karen Taylor Bass

TAYLORMADE BOOKS
Valley Stream, NY 11580-2219
www.karentaylorbass.com

Copyright © 2015, by Karen Taylor Bass. All rights reserved

Library of Congress Cataloging-in-Publication Data

No part of this book may be reproduced in any form or by any electronic or mechanical means including information storage and retrieval systems, without permission in writing from the author.

Contact *info@taylormademediapr.com* for more information.

Design & Production: Straight Design, **www.str8tdesign.com**

PRINTING: CreateSpace.com

FIRST PRINTING: September 2015

ISBN: 0-9759106-4-7

Table of Contents

Thank You

I WAS HIGH ON THE CLOUDS, danced, smiled and laughed. Then I tumbled (hard). You put me on your shoulder—carried me, loved me and inspired me. Humbled by my angels (earth and heaven), family and friends for never allowing me to settle.

I pressed RESET and you can too. Never stop until it feels right.

Create in me a clean heart, O God, and
renew a right spirit within me. —Psalm 51:10

30 DAY RESET:
Brand, Business & Bottom Line

Reset: Keep On Pushing Until It Feels Right

REAL TALK. Many entrepreneurs will fail at launching a business in less than 12 months.

According to TheRoot.com – Entrepreneurs starting a business grew 3 times (reported in 2013) the national rate, however, the challenge was staying in business longer than a year. Most people prepare to launch a business, but they do not create a plan to stay in business and compete. It's my passion to teach a client the magic of gaining media exposure while growing their brand, business and bottom-line with a strategy in 30 days. Yes. This can happen in 30 days. My book will show you how to create a goal and simply commit for 30 days (to start). Once you see the success of focusing on the goal and more importantly, doing the work consistently to stay in business, you will want to do more. Success does not happen overnight, but it will happen with consistency.

According to Webster's Dictionary, the word RESET, can be defined as, to set anew, fresh start, rewrite past mistakes, clean slate; basically, the ultimate 'aha' moment, when you have finally figured the "ish" that has been holding you back and keeping you life hostage.

If you are like me, I say welcome to the ultimate reset: your brand, business and bottom-line. This book is designed with you in mind, all the tools you need to stop co-starring in your life, and snag and accept your starring role. *I wanted to update 'You Want Caviar But Have Money For*

Chitlins' with a new title, cover, inspiring essays and renewed purpose to let you know that I, too, needed to press reset. I know for certain that everything that I've been through has prepared me for this opportunity. Yes. The opportunity to truly inspire entrepreneurs, while empowering them with the tools to breathe new life into their brand/business and more importantly, self. So, what does that mean? Unequivocally, that means that everything in life requires a plan. The minute you accept that notion and take the vision an extra mile, and define what you really want, how you want it, that you are tired of experiencing the pain – then you are really, really ready to press RESET?

I was not fully living up to my potential in my life, brand, business and self. You see – I always had the winning brand formula, however, wasn't ready to star in my own feature role. I am now.

I believe you are ready. This book will empower you to:
   1. Embrace failure. It's a necessary step to get to greatness
   2. Create a winning PR/marketing plan for your business
   3. Be realistic with goals
   4. Interact with select media/press via social/traditional media
   5. Network as if your life depends on it
   6. Understand and master the needs of your clients
   7. Welcome competition. We need it to thrive

Are you ready to accomplish your goal in 30, 60, 90 days with a consistent PR plan? I believe you are ready.

Here's to brand you!

Karen :)

Introduction

I TRULY BELIEVE THAT EVERYONE is a publicist at heart. Have you ever listened to the radio and wondered why certain songs are played more than others? Read the magazines and noticed that certain celebrities, socialites, and products are mentioned more than others? Those observations mark a publicist in training.

After almost twenty years of being a publicist I realized the importance of educating individuals on how to utilize PR to empower their lives. PR is free and when used effectively it can really work. Now it is crucial to remember that when applying the PR principles you must be patient because you have to be perpetually persistent, be on point with you message and realize that if you get a *NO* you must keep on trucking and try again. Get a thick skin and believe in yourself/product and keep it moving.

When success, timing, preparation, networking and blessings are aligned you are not going to believe how a dream, plan can change your life. I am introducing you to some of my friends in this guide. They have had small to galactic success but not before hitting rock bottom. Upon getting back up they *tweaked, re-focused* and *implemented* the Caviar & Chitlin mantra... Stay on course, stay on message—it's a matter of time before it's your time.

Be prepared and be positioned to make this work for you

Be on time

Be brief

Be prepared

Let your work speak for itself and don't feel ashamed to take credit

Be consistent

30 DAY RESET:
Brand, Business & Bottom Line

CHAPTER 1
The Power of PR

WHEN DID PUBLIC RELATIONS TAKE OVER THE WORLD?

Doesn't it seem that everyone is either PR savvy...or not savvy, at all? Is there no middle ground? There are professionals or celebrity "authorities" hawking products on every channel and many of us might wonder what they have that we don't. Well, the answer is, absolutely nothing.

As entrepreneurs, small business owners, and individuals with side-hustles, it is imperative that we understand the power of public relations and how to utilize strategic PR principles to be empowered and grow a successful enterprise. As a PR expert, I can admit that many of my clients didn't initially understand the power and value of public relations, but over time, we've begun to create new strategies, together.

In today's society, Public Relations can make-or-break a company. That said, there are 10 simple steps that I teach at my 'As Powerful As You Want To Be!'-PR Boot Camp, which can be put to use, right away, and take your company to the next level on a limited budget. Now, if you have an extra $3-5,000 to retain a publicist each month, you're on the fast track, but it never hurts to know how to do-it-yourself.

To move forward, it is essential to understand the difference between public relations and publicity-public relations is fostering public goodwill and creating a favorable opinion for a product, person or thing; publicity is simply the vehicle (i.e. TV, radio, magazine, newspaper, etc.), which brings attention to the product.

First, you must have a plan. You've got to be passionate, creative and strategic. Also, ask yourself a few questions. Where do you see your business-is it local, regional, national, global or virtual? What type of clients do you want to pursue and attract? Start believing in your hype, know that your story is unique and most important, talk yourself up to others like an A-List celebrity.

Here are 10 tips to implement as you create awareness and grow your business, right now:

1) Define Your Mission.

What is your company about? What are your objectives? Who is your target audience?

2) Be a Student of the Media.

Learn how the media works. For instance, be aware of who your desired outlet serves, what their deadlines are, when they publish or broadcast as well as their current trend for stories.

Ask yourself what makes your story different. Not all media outlets are appropriate for every type of business.

3) Be Prepared for the Opportunity.

Create a media kit, which consists of a press release announcing your company/product to seduce the media and entice clients to patronize your business, a biography (your life story, 1-2 pages with interesting information), a headshot for the media to run your photo and of course, a professional business card and website.

4) Think Linearly.

Act with a plan. Identify what you want to promote, the audience you want to reach, the tools you'll need (press release, etc), and media vehicles through which to accomplish your goal.

5) Promote yourself.

Brand you. Remember, you are an authority in your field, so begin to visualize, and execute your plan via public speaking engagements at schools, colleges, organizations, etc. Write an editorial or op-ed column, blog, appearance as a guest on local TV, public access, and/or talk radio. Network and work your magic every time.

6) Polish your image (outward and inward).

Are you sending out the message that you want? If so, what is that perception? Ask your friends and family members what impression they have of you.

7) Secure a Committed Mentor.

Make certain that the mentor you choose has time to be a mentor. Be clear with expectations and time and make it a two-way street. What do you have to offer? Also, be sure to give back to someone else who might be in need a mentor.

8) Create and Maintain Key Relationships.

Identify folks with common interests and different skills. Be a good friend and stand by your word.

9) Empower Your Life.

Give back. A great deal of business is done while volunteering, which can provide you a legitimate aura of leadership, dedication and commitment. Expand your base of key contacts. Become a board member and create a positive perception of who you are.

10) Honor Your Process, Believe Your Hype.

Remember, you are the best person for the job and you are entitled to success. PR is about knowing your worth and not underselling yourself to secure and/or maintain business.

The time to position yourself for an opportunity is now. Editors, TV bookers, publishers, online outlets are looking for original, inspiring and creative stories to capture each hour, day, week and month.

Get started and be your own publicist.

Reprinted from an article I wrote for The Network Journal, ***www.tnj.com***

Notes

Notes

30 DAY RESET:
Brand, Business
& Bottom Line

CHAPTER 2
Effective Messaging

SO, HERE IS WHERE YOU get the chance to really shine and put yourself out there. Having an effective message is what will propel you to superstardom. You must claim your power! Think about what is it that you want to say, how you want to say it and why people need to support your message and product. I will be using the word "product" to refer to a person and or thing.

The passion and ability to speak with power and clarity before a group—large or small—will take you to next level as you realize and actualize your goals of self-empowerment.

Here are a few suggestions to make you "win" at any time, place, and audience.

RESET MOMENT *Define and determine what makes you special and an authority on the subject?*

The Audience

■ Identify your audience, why are you targeting them?

■ Know everything there is about this group (taste, style, background, purchasing habit, income/education, ethnicity)

■ Location, Location, Location (why was this the chosen location? How did they travel via bus, train, car, carpool, plane)

■ When is your presentation scheduled? (morning, afternoon, evening) you will want to temper or amp up energy depending upon the time of your presentation. After work crowds generally need more stimulation and energy. Are you the only person presenting, if not, what is your time slot?

■ How much time do you have to set-up and perform your magic?

The Message

■ Believe in yourself. If you don't believe in you, no one else will.

■ Tell your story with honesty and hunger.

■ Think out your message like a good novel (what is the beginning, middle, and juicy end). *End on a positive.

■ Find an anecdote (short, funny, poignant personal story the audience can relate to)

■ Stick to the script. Write and rehearse before presentation.

■ Stay on message. If you are given 15 minutes, keep your time (longer doesn't mean better)

■ Passion. This can make or break your message. Show why you are the best person to pitch the product

■ What makes your product a "standout?"

■ Name 3-5 things that are beneficial about your product

■ Close the deal at the end. Sell, position yourself as an authority, plug product, website, special promotion

The Delivery

- Be Comfortable and remember posture is key

- Look engaging, address the audience with your name and fabulous credentials

- If there is a podium, don't stand behind it ... work the room and be personable

- Converse and captivate your audience, get them involved and make it personal

- Speak at a good pace and project ... don't rush your message

- Do you. Use your style and personality and work it

- Always reiterate your message and watch your time

- End strong and work it like a rock star

RESET MOMENT   *You will only excel if you practice, practice, practice and believe your words*

Notes

_____
_____
_____
_____
_____
_____
_____
_____
_____
_____
_____
_____
_____
_____
_____
_____
_____
_____
_____
_____
_____
_____
_____
_____

Notes

30 DAY RESET:
Brand, Business & Bottom Line

CHAPTER 3
Writing A Winning Press Release

YOU HAVE A LOT TO say and must say it well. You eagerly want people to read, cover, and write about your product/event. The goal is to write a sharp, engaging, call to action announcement about your product/event that will not be denied by members of press. The press release should do what it implies ... an interesting announcement (what are you announcing?) structured in the format of a news release with all the necessary information (who, what, where, when, why) for the press to (hopefully) salivate and be so inclined to contact you and commit to covering your story in the respective media outlet (newspaper, magazine, TV, blog, radio, cable).

RESET MOMENT

Press is free. Everyone and their momma are clamoring for publicity. You must bring the noise/drama/touch a heart to make your product STAND OUT.

My advice to you is real simple. There is not enough space to cover everything, so your press release must be engaging, informative, well written and have some philanthropic (cause-related) angle. People really want to feel good when they report a story. Also, sadly to say, most editors, journalists don't read beyond the 2nd paragraph. If you were planning on saving the best information for last in the release, dismiss that thought. Most writers/editors hate their jobs and are doing the very least, so you must make your release the best thing since slice bread. Come with the good fight in the first paragraph, put all the relative information and hook for the reader/editor in the beginning for consideration and coverage.

I am providing a guide to writing a dynamic press release by my friend and colleague, Chris Cathcart of One Diaspora Group (*chris@onedg.com*) based in Los Angeles, CA.

Writing and Using A Press Release : *By Chris Cathcart*

Don't let a limited marketing budget keep you from getting your project in front of the right people via the media. An effective public relations campaign does not have to cost a lot of money. And the press release is probably the most inexpensive form of publicity. However, if an editor doesn't pick up your release, you are most definitely getting what you paid for—nothing. A successful press release will have the following key elements:

1. **Strategic Placement** – Make sure it is targeted to the right media
2. **Relevant Content** – It must offer NEWS that the media considers important to its audience
3. **Proper Structure** – Your must adhere to professional standards in terms of form and structure (hint: the shorter the release, the better; it should be free of flowery language, over-hype, etc.)

It cannot be overstated that your press release must convey some form of real news, not an ego stroke, or a nice item of relevance only to you, your company or immediate circle. It must pass the "would the average consumer care about this" test. It is not an essay where you can wax poetic, it is a news story that reviews the facts…and nothing but the facts.

Based on your research, you should know which publications/outlets are most likely to find your story of interest, and the more you know about a publication the better. You should become a student of the media; know the differences between outlets, including their audiences and deadlines (the cut-off time for publications before they go to print for the next issue):

For Example

    Daily Newspapers *(deadlines are everyday, generally at the end of the work day)*

    Weekly Newspapers *(deadlines are the day before publication)*

    Monthly Magazines *(deadlines could be 2-3 months ahead of street date)*

    Weekly Magazines *(deadlines are the day before publication)*

    On-line services *(deadlines vary – do the research)*

Let's assume your press release has reached the right person. After the editor picks up your piece, you have about 10 seconds to grab his/her attention and make him/her care about your story. An editor acts as a screener of material for their "clients"– the readers or audience. He knows what they want and if he wants to keep them as clients, he has to give it to them. That keeps everybody – the reader, the publisher and the advertisers – happy.

So, you have to think like a newsperson and make the content relevant; and make the relevance obvious. In short, make the editor want to read on and, through that, share your news with his/her audience.

How to/Press Release

Obviously, if your press release does not go to the proper outlets, or convey relevant content, then the structure will matter little. However, let's assume you hit the mark on those points. How do you structure the information? Following are a few tips that are underscored by an actual press release the OneDiaspora Group prepared for a client, each of the following tips are illustrated on the sample.

1. Press Release should be on your letterhead

2. Contact information (name, phone number, email address) should appear at the top of the release (you should also repeat it at the end of the release).

3. It should be stated at the top that it's a press release and the release date.

4. The headline is your chance to catch the editor's interest. It is the angle of your story. Make it eye grabbing; the use of a sub-headline can also be effective, though not necessary. **The headline should be in bold type.**

5. The dateline includes the location and date of the press release; **this should be in bold as well.**

6. The first sentence of the of the first paragraph is called the "lead." It tells what the release is about; this sentence and the remainder of the first paragraph should answer as many WHO, WHAT, WHEN, WHERE, and HOW questions as possible.

7. Middle paragraphs should continue to answer the key questions (if necessary) as well as offer quotes from authorities/key parties (usually you or who you are representing) explaining why the news is important to the readers/audience. Middle paragraphs also summarize and further detail the facts, issues, persons discussed in the release, etc.

8. The final paragraph should always be the "boilerplate," a concise statement about your firm's/group's services and mission (very important in promoting yourself; you should draft a standard paragraph that can be used over and over again).

9. Repeat contact information–very important if the publication runs your release in its entirety–which many small outlets do.

10. End each release with # # # in the middle of the page.

Here's a helpful hint…press releases and news stories read very much alike. Start paying closer attention to how the articles in your favorite newspapers are written; check out the leads, how information is introduced, and the transition from one paragraph to another, etc.

SAMPLE PRESS RELEASE

OneDiaspora Group _____ **1**
Press Release

PRESS RELEASE
For Immediate Release
Tuesday, September 12, 2000

2

3

CONTACT:
Chris Cathcart/OneDiaspora
323/850-8982
onediaspora@earthlink.net

MEDIAWORKS ADVERTISING SECURES $3 MILLION CAMPAIGN FOR ABC ATHLETIC SHOES

4

AGENCY PRODUCES NATIONAL TV SPOTS AND COORDINATES GRAND OPENINGS AND SUSTAINING MARKET PROMOTIONS FOR FOOTWEAR RETAILER

5

6

Los Angeles, CA – Sept. 12, 2000 — Displaying its ability to meet a general market client's integrated marketing needs, MediaWorks Advertising Inc. (MWA), the nation's premiere multicultural marketing and advertising agency, has completed three 30-second television spots for ABC Athletic Shoes "Work Out Now" promotion. The media campaign, with billings estimated at $3 million, marks MWA's second general market project for the athletic footwear company.

"Relationships are key in every aspect of business," says J.D. Hamilton, chairman and executive creative director of MediaWorks Advertising Inc. "Based on the success of our previous work with ABC, they approached us about handling their annual campaign. We jumped at the opportunity."

7

The taggable TV ads provide ABC corporate, franchise and international stores with commercials appropriate for use in the top 50 metropolitan markets. The three spots revolve around ABC's "Work Out Now" campaign and feature everyday people participating in a variety of sports and fitness activities with a musical cadence that accentuates the " Work Out Now " message.

The agency also coordinated all the advertising and event sustaining market promotions for the grand openings of 17 corporate locations throughout the country. MWA began producing the store openings in the fourth quarter of 1999 and continued through this year, with more planned for the coming months.

ABC Athletic Shoes, Inc. is a privately owned international athletic footwear retailer, operating more than 800 corporate and franchise stores in 40-plus countries. Founded in 1991, the Plainfield, NJ-based company is a subsidiary of Unit First, a retail conglomerate with interests in fashion, home improvement, sports and real estate.

8

Founded in 1984, MWA has vast experience in developing integrated marketing programs to reach America's diverse consumers. Its clients include America Honda, The President's Anti-Drug Media Campaign, The Centers for Disease Control, Health Care Finance Administration, and Mandalay Bay Resort and Casino, among others.

MediaWorks Advertising Inc. is the nation's first and only minority-owned marketing and communications holding company. Along with MWA, its properties include The Darren Anita Group, a New York City-based multicultural strategic consulting firm, and Riptide Research, a premiere multicultural research company.

For more information, please contact Chris Cathcart at 323/850-8982 or Chris@OneDG.com.

9

10 ———— # # #

Note: Information below is not a part of the official press release.

This sample release is for instructional use only, not to be distributed for any other purpose; the information detailed above is entirely fictional.

© 2000 Christopher Cathcart and The OneDiaspora Group. All Rights Reserved.

Chris Cathcart, author, PR consultant and speaker, The One Diaspora Group based in Los Angeles. www.onediaspora.com.

Notes

_____
_____
_____
_____
_____
_____
_____
_____
_____
_____
_____
_____
_____
_____
_____
_____
_____
_____
_____
_____
_____
_____
_____

Notes

_____
_____
_____
_____
_____
_____
_____
_____
_____
_____
_____
_____
_____
_____
_____
_____
_____
_____
_____
_____
_____
_____
_____
_____
_____
_____
_____

30 DAY RESET:

Brand, Business & Bottom Line

CHAPTER 4

Positioning Yourself for an Opportunity

YOU WANT IT SO BAD ... you can taste, drink, and see your success. Are you ready for success? Is your team in place? Many times people are not prepared for the avalanche of blessings when they occur, please be ready. Here are a few tips to get you started:

1.   **Be prepared.** Success can smell success. Have that look about you, dress appropriately, and have your message on hand to deliver the pitch and close the deal. If you believe in your product others will come to the party in a matter of time.

2.   **Reputation is everything.** Let you work and rep speak for you. If you give your word, honor it. Don't commit if you cannot meet deadline – people always remember the screw up.

3.   **Be outspoken.** If you don't agree with someone's agenda or how they are positioning your product speak up. Being amenable to everything will not garner fans, only enemies down the line.

4.   **Be well rounded**. Make certain that you are always briefed on current events; this will empower you to have a conversation with any CEO, mogul or average Joe.

5.   **Be proactive.** If there is someone that you want to get in contact with–reach out. Write a letter, send an email, make a call, look within your circle for a connection. Work in that order and you will get results.

6.   **Never too busy.** Time is a premium and you are a priority. Make certain that you treat yourself and others that way. If someone is reaching out to you, then you must respond in a timely fashion. Karma is everything.

7.   **Get to know the "team."** Don't be an elitist and ignore the administrative assistant, reception, mailroom clerks, etc. They are the

ones really running the company and are privy to information. Say hello to everyone and become allies with those in the "know" don't get confused with office trappings (corner office, title, expense account).

8. Be Wacky to stand out. Make your own rules. Send Christmas/Holiday cards in June; Valentine Cards in December. Set your own tone and be noticed.

9. Stay out of gossip. Don't get caught up not minding your business, which means not taking care of your money. If you have an opinion, speak directly to the respective party you have an "issue" with.

10. Dream vampires. I would not advise you to share your dream with people unless they are like - minded and posses the same energy as you. Record your dreams in a journal and talk with God.

11. Network and utilize your connection. I don't know why we always forget to tap into our database and circle. Join organizations to widen your networking base and utilize your friends/co-workers/affiliation to make the introduction for you.

12. Empower yourself and others. Real simple – give back to others from a sacred space and be counted. You can volunteer, make a contribution or there just be for someone in need.

13. Be consistent. If you provide service a certain way ... continue to provide it that same way, only better.

14. Be Viral. The Internet is a force and you must participate. For companies to prosper they must register with an online social network for connections (LinkedIn, Twitter, MySpace, Facebook); blog; e-blast newsletters; webinars; podcast.

15. Smile and look engaging.

RESET MOMENT *Get out there and be counted. Be purposeful, be poised, and be consistent.*

Trust, Believe & Sparkle : *by Sandy Baker*

Real talk: We all need weekly motivation to stay committed, forgive self and allow the universe to work. As an entrepreneur, I've learned that staying encouraged, creating a new road map and walking into your destiny is the only way to sparkle.

Meet Sandy Baker. Her name might not be familiar to you (yet), but her jewelry has adorned the likes of Julia Roberts, Natalie Cole, the late Dr. Maya Angelou and FLOTUS, Michelle Obama.

Baker has been an artist and tinkerer as far back as she can remember. Beginning in childhood with pencils and crayons, she soon moved on to Popsicle sticks, aluminum foil, colored tape, paint and clay, then to steel dapping tools, hammers, a jewelers bench block, a soldering torch and a flexible shaft. Being a Black woman in the jewelry industry has not always been easy for her, but she never gave up the vision to have her jewelry sold in stores, shown in galleries, museums, and magazines and celebrated by both famous and everyday people.

Recently, I interviewed Sandy Baker about finding one's voice, inspiration and pressing #RESET (marinate on her answers in this format).

How did you discover your passion?
Sandy Baker: As a teenager I felt the need to express myself creatively and I could not find jewelry that outwardly reflected my sensibilities, so I decided to start making my own. When I started there were few women in the fine jewelry industry, and no women of color, which meant I had to fight to secure my position. As I progressed to being a manufacturing jeweler selling to stores, I knew it meant that I could show women that the distribution of our creative products can go beyond friends, family and the neighborhood.

When you entered the jewelry industry and no one looked liked you, what became your mindset/mantra?
SB: My mindset was picturing my bold, unique, wearable art on bold and unique women of all walks of life. I saw the vision and believed it. Giving up was not an option.

What classes, workshops and conferences helped you to develop/hone your craft?

SB: I took jewelry classes in college and in graduate school. I attended various fashion shows, jewelry shows, so I could see what was out there. Also, I registered for classes and workshops in the summer to learn and fine-tune specific skills-stone setting, bezel making and silversmithing. It was then that I made the decision, to sell my creations to stores and not individuals.

What was the initial investment for launching Sandy Baker Art?

SB: It was around $7,000 to invest in supplies, manufacturing, traveling to find precious gems, marketing and networking.

How important was marketing/branding in getting the message out there about your art?

SB: Marketing and branding was exceedingly important. My early slogan was "Sandy Baker does ears like nobody else." The first 10 years of my business, I did only earrings. I focused on getting stores to look at my collection if they wanted something besides hoops and love knots.

My goal was to be the "Queen of earring design." I had T-shirts, tote bags, gift cards that went with each purchase that told the purchaser about me. The gift cards with my picture and bio were free to the stores. Also, my logo has evolved over the years because I've also evolved.

Why do you call your work art, not jewelry?

SB: My art is unique and artfully created and produced in limited editions. Many pieces are more sculpture than just jewelry. I love designing forms that work in three-dimensional space. My earrings in particular come to life when someone is wearing them. My designs play with positive and negative space-the face, the jaw line, the space below the ear and light.

Biggest challenge to date?

SB: How much time do you have? Ha. I would say infringement of my intellectual property has been the biggest challenge. Technology has made it easier for people to replicate, and in some cases steal my designs. Sometimes I see modified versions of designs that I did 20 and 30 years ago being sold in stores today made out of cheaper materials.

How did you press RESET?

SB: Throughout my career I have had to continually press RESET. From keeping up with current fashion trends, to adjusting to the rising costs of raw materials, and modifying my price points accordingly. I started out working in 18K gold, 14K gold and sterling silver. I then moved to sterling silver exclusively. Later, I moved to designing my own color inlays in place of standard commercial semi-precious stones. I use more organic materials these days like South Sea blue-green abalone.

Biggest accomplishment to date?

SB: I feel my biggest accomplishment has been the opportunity to reach so many women with my work, and create pieces that they cherish. Currently my work is included in a traveling jewelry exhibition by the American Jewelry Design Council. The show originally opened at the Forbes Galleries in New York. Selections from my work are included in the Design Archives of the Smithsonian. [And] my work has been published.

What would you tell the person reading this article that feels like it will never happen for them?

SB: They must know that life and their dreams and aspirations do not necessarily travel in a straight line. Stay focused, reach far and believe. Never allow minor obstacles to derail your destiny.

RESET: *Stay true to your vision, and never settle for anything less than walking into your purpose.*

Sandy Baker is the first African-American Female jewelry designer recognized nationally and internationally. You can see her jewelry at ***sandybakerjewelry.com***

Notes

_____
_____
_____
_____
_____
_____
_____
_____
_____
_____
_____
_____
_____
_____
_____
_____
_____
_____
_____
_____
_____
_____
_____

Notes

_____

_____

_____

_____

_____

_____

_____

_____

_____

_____

_____

_____

_____

_____

_____

_____

_____

_____

_____

_____

_____

_____

_____

_____

_____

_____

30 DAY RESET:
Brand, Business & Bottom Line

CHAPTER 5
Branding Yourself Like Nobody's Business

IN TODAY'S SOCIETY BRANDING IS a word that is over-used and most people don't really know what it is. Real simple – branding is a consistent message about your product and its uniqueness. For example, TaylorMade Media is known for creating innovative PR campaigns, offering consultation and "thinking out of the box." Each campaign is "tailored" for its uniqueness. Regardless of company size, it is imperative to make your product stand out, define and accept your niche and position you/company as an "expert" in the field. Be creative, design your campaign as if you were a $20 million a picture box-office star. Pretend the sky is the limit and utilize your imagination and connection. Score public appearances, guest appearance on TV/cable, public access, writing editorials/columns, blogging and mail personalized cards, etc.

RESET MOMENT

If you believe that your product is the best in the field, go after it with passion, trust and God's blessing.

My husband, Andrew Bass, is a multi-award-winning graphic designer. In addition to having a full-time position, he also has his own freelance consultancy, Straight Design (*www.str8tdesign.com*). His essay can help one transform their business.

Branding Is Not Just for Big Guns : *Andrew Bass*

The use of brand and branding has become the catch phrase for businesses in the 21st century. But exactly what does that mean?

Simply put, a brand is the unique business, product or service that you bring to the market. Branding is the action in which you apply that uniqueness across all items related to that brand. It becomes the strategy of how you make your brand and its customers relate to one another. When folks talk about brand and branding, Fortune 500 companies are usually mentioned in the same breath. Most small businesses believe creating a brand is out of their reach. Most small businesses think of branding as a luxury expense that they believe they can't afford.

Wrong, wrong, wrong. Nothing can be further from the truth. All businesses have a brand. What they have to figure out is what makes it different from the rest of your competition. Branding can benefit ALL companies no matter their size. By careful planning, prioritizing what is needed and aligning yourself with dependable vendors, you can create a branding system for your business at a lower cost than you think.

Branding has become a big business in itself. There are different philosophies and many methods on how to create an effective branding campaign. What I'm sharing is a straight to the point outline of what is needed to begin branding your business.

So Where Do I Begin?

You have your brand (your business, product or service). Now you have to figure what exactly separates your brand from similar brands. What is your unique selling point? An example of this would be Nike which is known as the company of "Just Do It." It represents the feelings of action, adventure, and being unafraid. Everything connected to Nike exemplifies that. So you have to figure out your unique selling point. Once you do that a strategy can be developed to have all the components of your brand, showcase that unique selling point. This is how you begin establishing your brand.

The next step in the branding process is making sure your strategy is applied consistently through all the components and extensions of your brand. There are constant elements that help make your brand more recognizable to potential customers and fellow businesses. Elements such as your identity (which is explained a little later), your colors, your images, your words, or your slogan become linked to your brand. All your tools, which I will discuss next, along with any extensions of your brand, advertising, promotions and so on must always contain linked elements. If your brand uses the colors of gray and orange with a slogan, then your website and advertising would use gray and orange with a slogan. This just reinforces your brand exposure to customers. Repeated exposure is how FedEx or Xerox has become part of our lexicon.

You have identified your brand. You have figured out your unique selling point. You now have a branding strategy. Let's look at the tools you will need for the next step.

Building That Brand

You'll need some basic working tools.

All businesses, no matter how big or how small will need these basic working tools if you want to stand out from your competitors and be a beacon for potential customers. There are other tools you can develop later on as your brand grows but for now, it is wise to do some long-term investing to try and profit in the short term.

The first tool you need is a face to your brand. You'll need what's called an identity or more commonly known as a logo. An identity can consist of a wordmark (which is just type chararcters, numerals and/or punctuation marks), a symbol or graphical image or a combination of both. This identity becomes the face for your brand and it must reflect the essence of what that brand is. You don't want to leave your house with your face all crusty and unkempt while the rest of you looks sharp as a tack. The same goes for your "brand identity."

Many companies today have an identity that gives off the wrong impression of what kind of business they are running. Just as you would think about how your personal appearance is, you must give the same sort of attention to your business's appearance.

The second tool will be a letterhead, envelope and business card. These tools are how you will communicate on a daily basis with customers and other companies. Say you meet someone one day and after you two get to talking, the other person asks for a business card. If you don't have one, are you going to write your business phone on some stray paper? How do you think that makes your look professionally? You know how—like a joke. The same goes for the letterhead and envelope. As a business, you send out correspondence every day from invoices to inquiry letters. You're not going to write it on just anything, right? Of course not.

The third tool needed will be a website. Why a website? In today's world, the Net allows you access to places all around the globe. Everyone wants instant constant nowadays and having a website provides that. Also, having a website allows you to have an email address that reflects your business name which is called a domain name. Free email services like Yahoo, AOL, Earthlink and Hotmail are great for personal emails but having a business email will let customers and other businesses know that you are serious. Which email address would you respond to johndoe@yahoo.com or johndoe@mycompanyworks.com?

At one time having a website was a costly proposition. Not today. With thousands of Internet Service Providers (ISP), you can get great monthly deals with a lot of features such as 2-gigabyte mailboxes, multiple email boxes and preset templates for easier self-building. Yahoo and Earthlink offer business hosting plans in addition to personal email services but they are not for free although they charge low monthly fees.

The fourth tool needed is a brochure that sells your brand. The identity is your brand's face, the stationery system are your clothes, the website are your arms and the brochure is your body. With a brochure, you can sell your brand with words and images that potential customers can actually hold and feel. It can be as complex as you want, it can be as lavish as you want or it can be a simple, as you want.

Trust me, it still makes a difference to potential customers (and competitors) when they can hold and feel something tangible of your brand. For now, the virtual world won't completely replace printed promotions because of our need for tactile stimulation.

Hire A Graphic Designer, Please

Just because you have a computer and they sell tons of do-it-yourself graphics doesn't mean you can now design your own branded graphics. Just because your niece likes art doesn't mean she can design your brand's graphics. Creating a coordinated system of graphics that fall in sync with the soul of your brand takes time, research, thought, lots of ideas—some trash, some great—and skill. Hire a graphic designer, please! Your brand will thank you.

Graphic design is now becoming a known profession thanks in part to TV shows and movies. Graphic designers are trained by degree in the principles of design that really becomes part science and part artistic impression. When hiring a graphic designer to help give your brand a visual life, he/she will work in tandem with you on how your brand is conveyed creating a unique look all to yourself. Most graphic designers have honed their skill by working with other businesses developing their graphic systems. You want to work with a graphic designer that has had solid working experiences.

But a word of caution—just like all professions not everyone is as competent as they claim. **Do** check their background. **Do** talk to their past clientele. **Do** ask to see a real live portfolio. I personally have seen some so-called designers pass off someone else's work as their own.

Be aware of the numerous design "chop" shops that offer to do logos for $59, brochures and postcards for $199 and so. These places promise numerous ideas and unlimited revisions on projects because they have large numbers of "artists" to work on your project. What they don't tell you is that your project will be from a prefabricated template that Acme Made Bakery in Anytown, USA also uses. No self-respecting graphic designer will churn out 20 to 30 ideas with an unlimited amount of revisions for any dollar amount. That is not productive for the designer and certainly not productive for your brand or business.

Many factors go into the pricing of developing a branded identity. The designer has to take into account the complexity of the brand, its message, how it will be applied, where it will be applied, and what other components will be added to it and other details. As each end result is uniquely different so is its fee structure. For example, fees for completing a branding system can range from $6,000 to $50,000 as a small business. But keep in mind the designer customizes his/her fee based on the details of the project as well as the size of the business.

Design "chop" shops don't follow the principles of design nor do they calculate all the factors that go into development but rather they are modeled like an assembly line—cheap, repetitive models—that is why their fees seem so "reasonable." What you receive is nothing of a unique character or perspective that will be related to your brand and quite possibly you may see your brand on some other company one day.

The old saying is true—you get what you pay for. Hiring a graphic designer or a graphic design studio will cost much more than $59 but you can be certain you will have hired someone who is skilled in graphic design, someone who is concerned how your brand will look and most of all someone who will give you that unique and original perspective that your brand deserves.

Let's Get This Started

Congratulations! You decided to hire a graphic designer. So now, where do you find one. Do you look in the yellow pages? The web? Ask around? Actually you can do all three. The yellow pages can provide you names of individual designers or design studios but depending on where you're based the listings may be slim. The best places are the web and referrals from other businesses. On the web you can do a local search for graphic design. Go through the listings and visit their websites for information. Your search doesn't have to be contained to local areas. Try different cities, around you even different states.

Visit graphic design organization sites such as **American Institute of Graphic Arts** (www.aiga.org) and **Graphic Artists Guild** (www.gag.org) to search their member directories. You can also check out *The Workbook Phonebook*, an on-line directory of artists including graphic design studios (www.workbook.com/phonebook) that covers all of the US, Canada and outside the USA.

Another great resource is referrals from businesses you admire. Ask them whom did they go to for help. If your friends have their own businesses, ask who helped them in developing their brand. Listen to what they have to say about their experience. Get as much information as you can before meeting with anyone.

Hopefully this helps make it easier to understand what a brand is, the importance of branding and the value of hiring a graphic designer or studio to help create your brand identity. It is all about using the same tools as the big guns but without the high cost. Just as we know customers are what ultimately makes a business thrive, having all the right tools at your disposal definitely puts you on a more fruitful path.

Andrew Bass is Design Strategist for Straight Design LLC, his award-winning freelance graphic design consultancy. His graphic expertise spans over 20 years creating winning logos, brochures, annual reports and magazines for many small business and not-for-profit clientele. His work has been recognized by GD:USA, The Ozzies and ASBPE. He's a member of AIGA and was an adjunct lecturer in the Art & Advertising Design Department at New York City College of Technology.

Notes

_____
_____
_____
_____
_____
_____
_____
_____
_____
_____
_____
_____
_____
_____
_____
_____
_____
_____
_____
_____
_____
_____
_____
_____
_____

Notes

30 DAY RESET:
Brand, Business & Bottom Line

CHAPTER 6
Work Your Magic, You Have The Goods

IT SEEMS VERY EASY WHEN you hear professionals talk about making the pitch and scoring a booking, placement, tear sheet for their respective product. I know that scoring media placement is not an easy fete, especially when there is less editorial space and lack of advertising support for the respective outlet. You are competing for space, positioning, and voice. Your product/story has to be unique, interesting and impactful. If you can add a social element of change, or a call to action you will have a better chance of being heard. When contacting the media, I always stress that you must be a student of the media. Before you start to pitch, consult 5 friends and inquire what makes your product interesting and different. Really listen to them so you can hone your pitch and practice first before making a call to a reporter, editor, TV booker, and so on.

Create a dynamic and engaging press release that will describe and convey the uniqueness of your product.

RESET MOMENT *Most editors/reports/bookers only read the first 2 paragraphs of the press release. Make certain you seduce the reader to go beyond the first 2 paragraphs.*

Learn and understand how the media works, who they serve (target audience), deadlines, when they publish, broadcast, what are bylines. The best way to get a handle is to spend time at your local library, newsstand, Barnes & Noble, Border, etc. Read with passion so you can understand that daily newspaper have deadlines each day; monthly magazines work 3 months ahead (so if you are calling for coverage on a special event in

December you must call them in August for consideration). Viral outlets, like the Internet are becoming more coveted so make certain that you utilize blogs, YouTube, professional networks (Twitter, Facebook) to get the word out and pitch your company to a viral audience.

Making That Pitch : *By Marcia Cole*

In this chapter I will focus on why certain press releases/pitches are printed or lead to feature stories. It all depends on what type of story is being pitched. But as a general rule, editors use the following criteria for following up on a pitch. Is there legitimacy to what's being pitched, meaning is there truth that is of value, or is it all hype, or worse yet, hype that you've heard before. In other words whatever is being pitched must have a point of differentiation that is unique, exclusive, and fits with the magazine's mission. Is it relevant to our readers, will it be a must-read? Is it coverline worthy? This last question is crucial if you want a bigger feature. Is this a time-sensitive issue, or is it an evergreen idea that can work at any time?

These are the questions we ask. Then, after more research is done, it's determined what to do.

How do you create a pitch?

Research the magazine's mission. Read the magazine and be creative with ideas. Refer to the criteria of your pitch being different, for each magazine. Meaning, don't pitch an interview with an artist and you and the other magazine spend your day at the spa. There is nothing worse for an editor than to have the same set up of a story appear in a competitor's title. This reduces the credibility of the publicist to nil.

Pointers in making a cold call?

Cold calls are hard, so find a way to break the ice. Introduce yourself with an email first. And when you're on the telephone with someone you don't know, get to the point. Quickly. Seriously. Make friendly conversation about the topic and adjust yourself to their vibe.

What are the essential elements needed?

Does emailing yield better results? How would a novice approach an editor? Are there certain key words, phrases? You must research and decide.

Is length important in a pitch letter?

I would keep it short and sweet, with a cute, eye-catching headline.

Is there a format to follow?

I don't think there is a format to follow. However, I do think the more creative, the better. Editors receive tons of mail and most don't sift through them the day it's delivered. Ask for honest feedback about the project, if they don't want to do anything with it, so that you'll know the next time. But the more you show you know about the sections(s) an editor oversees or the magazine in general, and the item you're pitching, the better your position.

---

*Marcia A. Cole is a 19-year magazine veteran with four years of interactive experience. She is the founder of **AMBERmag.com**.*

Notes

Notes

_____
_____
_____
_____
_____
_____
_____
_____
_____
_____
_____
_____
_____
_____
_____
_____
_____
_____
_____
_____
_____
_____
_____

Notes

_____
_____
_____
_____
_____
_____
_____
_____
_____
_____
_____
_____
_____
_____
_____
_____
_____
_____
_____
_____
_____
_____
_____
_____
_____
_____
_____
_____

30 DAY RESET:
Brand, Business & Bottom Line

CHAPTER 7
Bring The Noise...Getting Your Product Out There

THE MARKET HAS CHANGED EXPONENTIALLY since I started TaylorMade Media in 1999. Having a business was always a dream of mine, however, I really never had all the specifics together until now. When I started my business it was purely out of necessity...I hated my job, hence started my own operation. When TMM opened its doors, it was in my living room in my spacious 1 bedroom apartment. Since I had just come off the very hot D'Angelo project as his publicist and chief "buzz" creator I was receiving offers from all over. I decided to take my chance and put out feelers to my friends about working as an independent music consultant/publicist for them. Well, in moments I was on the receiving end...clients, projects, and bidding wars. I loved being in demand and simply started to work and hired an executive assistant to help me manage my calendar, and business.

How do you grow, when you really don't want to?

Word of mouth was everything for my business. TMM delivered and our clients sang our praises and business continued to grow. I must say through it all I must have opened and closed TMM 3 times. Sending out promotional materials to executives helped to put TMM on the radar, however, I was never strategic enough to promote myself and business. I did not write a marketing plan or position myself as an authority in Public Relations. This would bite me later on when I decided I wanted to re-invent myself.

Learning from your mistakes.

I am skipping over a lot of the details because you can google me;

visit taylormademediapr.com to learn my story. This book is very important because I made so many mistakes in the beginning, not taking my business seriously, not identifying my niche, not positioning myself for an opportunity, not leveraging my clients, and most of all, not believing or understanding my POWER. Now that I am in the middle and have a serious marketing/pr plan, amazing team, office space, and a dynamite vision from GOD I am doing it the right way. Not to mention...I have fallen and cracked my face over and over in recent years and I want to spare you all the dreaded mistakes. *Some steps to announce a business, listed below:*

- Send out a press release (4) weeks prior to local papers, online outlets, bloggers
- Offer VIP coupons to business/community editors at respective papers
- Enlist your family, friends, organization to assist you in spreading the word
- Promote the event by distributing flyers, and use bright colors to attract attention
- Invest in unique giveaways
- Invite the local radio station to broadcast live from you event (especially if there is a community angle)
- Invite local/area celebrity to participate
- Utilize the barter system. Partner with companies that can help you provide a service
- Hire good looking people to promote your event, wear t-shirts, pass out flyer
- Follow up on the press release (2) weeks prior to the event to secure coverage
- Try your best to keep your word and deadlines
- Word of mouth is everything
- Forget about thinking "outside the box" – knock down the box
- Believe in your product

Marketing A Grassroots Empire : By Syretta Scott

Like many entrepreneurs, the rapid success of my natural hair care business is undoubtedly linked to a shift in social values that helped create a space for more African identified forms for beauty to reemerge and flourish. In 2000, as the New-Soul Movement expanded, I was quick to develop a robust client base among the spoken-word poets, artists, musicians and singers on the local Philadelphia scene. As the audience grew, so did an appreciation of natural hairstyles such as lock and traditional braiding. At the time, there were very few locally based natural hair salons and I was able to accommodate what can best be described as a niche market.

Initially, I made house calls to service my client needs but soon after, established a makeshift salon within the confines of my mother's living room to support an expanding clientele. **Duafe Holistic Hair Care** was born. As an entrepreneur, it was extremely important for me to behave in a proactive manner.

By writing a mission statement, I clearly identified a market and determined how to best position my business with that market. I also understood the intrinsic value of brand recognition with an emerging marketplace. Therefore, I immediately established a trade logo and began an aggressive marketing campaign to reach others within the larger African American community, who desired a more natural aesthetic but had limited options.

In order to publicize **Duafe**, I produced a series of advertisement fliers, which were strategically posted in vegetarian restaurants, health food stores, and other black-owned businesses frequented by more progressive, culturally conscious people ready to transition back to natural hairstyles. I continued to develop a significant presence on the alternative music scene by attending concerts and spoken word events, where I distributed business cards, fliers and t-shirts as promotional tools. In addition, I attracted many new clients by providing a reliable, dependable service and building strong relationships that encouraged word-of-mouth referrals.

How do you expand a business?

Business expansion is dependent on two distinct factors. Most important, is the stability of the business itself. As the owner of **Duafe Holistic Hair Care**, it is my responsibility to manage business operations and further advance the standards of service associated with the salon by hiring polite and dependable staff. Customers continue to support our business because we provide a clean, comfortable and professional service in an Afrocentric environment. Customer intimacy has always been the primary focus of **Duafe**. Our signature services have bee further enriched by our offerings of extended hours and flexible appointment schedules. We maintain close client relationships though thank you cards as well as promotional postcards and magnets. We also feature actual clients in our advertisements.

The second critical aspect of business expansion is the ability to reinvest in the business. As the owner of a natural hair salon, I invested a considerable amount of time and research to learn and teach the practices and techniques of traditional African hairstyles to recreate more accessible everyday wear. By the same token, I have reinvested my profits in the business by breaking the renter's cycle and becoming a property owner. Four years after having started my business in my mother's living room, I now own the building where **Duafe Holistic Hair Care** now exists. The money that I would have ordinarily spent on rent, I can now reinvest in technology to better manage our client database and website. I also have funds available to increase my advertising base and cross the boundaries of race to reach an entirely new clientele.

Syreeta Scott is the proprietor of Duafe Holistic Hair Care based in Philadelphia, PA. Visit ***www.du-afe.com***.

Book Publishing—From A to Z : *By Pam Perry*

If you talk to any author, they will tell you that writing their book was the easy part – compared to marketing it and getting folks to buy it!

You can go to any bookstore and get a book on how to publish your book or do a Google search on book publishing. (I recommend Dan Poynter's *Self-Publishing Manual* – he's been called the guru of self-publishing). You can even get a good editor to help you with your rough manuscript. If you really don't want to do that much work and want to get your book out fast, you can go to "iuniverse.com" or "lulu.com" and have books produced, as you needed. This is called Print-On-Demand (POD) – great for first time authors; they take your word document and turn it into a book. Kinkos is even in the book producing game.

The production of a book is now pretty common. That's why we see so many people doing books.

But are the books selling? After the books are back from the printer/ publisher – the real work begins. It's time to promote and sell your book. You have just opened up a business. Like any new business, you need a business plan plus extensive knowledge of the field you're in and good advisors. A standard statistic you need to know according to book industry sources: there are over 150,000 new books published every year. And typically we see the same roster of authors on the *New York Times* Best-Seller's list.

As a book publicist for over ten years in the Christian literary field, I see what flys and what fizzles. Before you embark on this costly venture (prepare to spend at least $2,500 up to $10,000 for editing, production and promotion), I would like to share with you what I've learned on what makes a best-seller:

- **Title** – is it griping, interesting? Would one know what it's about without reading anything else?
- **Cover** – people do judge a book by its cover. Make sure it has enough punch to stand out on the shelves among the thousands of other books Is it clean, neat and crisp– yet interesting? Hire a professional!
- **Endorsements** – what others say about you is key. Who these people are is even more important. Pull together the "best words from the best people." It will pre-sell your book before you even open your mouth.

- **Writer's credentials** – do you have anything else with your byline? Do you blog? Do you have an audience that actually likes what you write?

- **Knowledge of the Market the book will reach** – and the author's reputation in that market. The author must create a market for himself by really addressing the needs of that market, knowing that market and communicating the right message to that market.

- **Timing** – in relation to other events going on in the world/society. Are there movies, songs or talk shows that are bringing up the subject you have discussed in your book? Do you read the newspaper regularly and respond with Opinion Editorials when they are discussing "your" platform/topic?

- **Advertising** – targeting the right message to the right media at the right time. Consistently!

- **Media coverage** – publicity. The frosting on the cake. Getting on radio, TV and in newspapers and magazine and Ezines. Consistently (with advertising too).

- **Distribution** – If you want to be a best-seller you have to have your book available. Make sure you sign up with a distributor or wholesaler so it is accessible to bookstores. (Amazon is not national distribution… it is a website) Best-sellers are sold in real bookstores and they only order from distributors or wholesales. (See Sally Stuart's Christian Writers Market Guide for distributors to approach. Note: You must have a press kit and solid marketing plan for them to consider you).

- **Word of Mouth** – The best advertising. The more "buzz" you have about your book the better. How do you get people talking about your book? By engaging in their culture and creating messages in their media. Be relentless in your goal to be a "best-seller" – and it will happen if you commit to the publicity process and pray for favor.

---

*Pam Perry is a ministry marketing pioneer and expert in the African American Christian market. Her company, Ministry Marketing Solutions Inc., has a roster of some of the most well known Christian publishers and African American Christian authors in the industry. For more information, go to **www.MinistryMarketingSolutions.com** and sign up for free PR tips.*

Notes

Notes

Notes

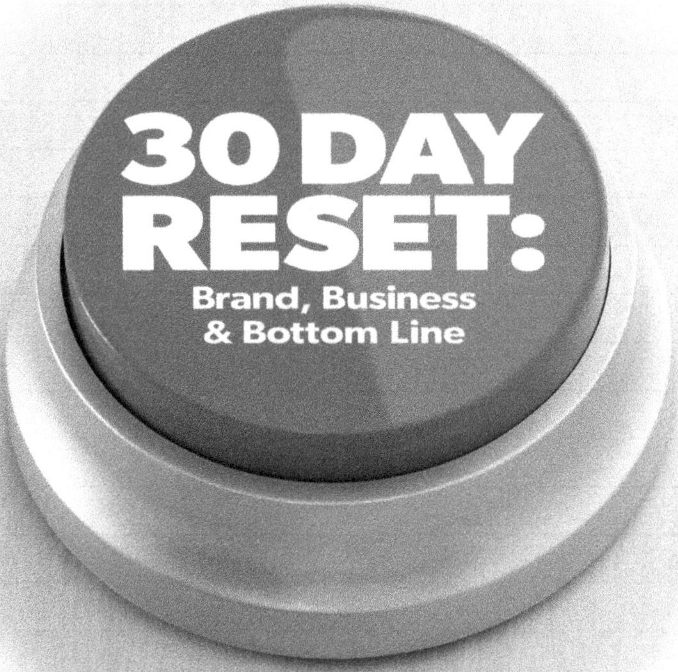
30 DAY
RESET:
Brand, Business
& Bottom Line

CHAPTER 8
Impressions, Impressions, Impressions...It's All Hype

CLAIM YOUR POWER.

You must believe that you deserve to live your best life everyday and always. Be creative, use your mouth in a positive, constructive and thoughtful manner. Tell everyone what you are doing, talk up your product to any and everyone that will listen, visualize it all happening and just do it.

I trust the power of God and the artform of viral communication — word of mouth. Combined together they are beyond powerful and free. It is at no cost to you to have a relationship with your God and, the same for word of mouth. The press will tell you no, over and over but, if you get creative and develop a fanbase, database, grassroots movement ala Tyler Perry, Barack Obama, and countless of others you can't lose. It just takes time and patience. I want to share a story with you my experience about securing a media booking for Jill Scott, a friend and past client.

When I started the Jill Scott movement, as a strategist/publicist the media was not checking for Jill. I was told repeatedly that Jill would not make it in the music industry, she was too big, music was too authentic and Black radio would not play it. They were right in the fact that Black radio had stopped taking risks; she actually had talent and most importantly, was big, bold and beautiful. I was determined to make the naysayer eat their words for breakfast, lunch and dinner.

I along with Hidden Beach Recordings created the best viral campaign for a musical artist. We pioneered the "Who Is Jill Scott?" movement— t-shirts, postcards, concerts, pre-blogging via social Internet sites, organizations, and Ms. Jill supplying the beautiful vocals and music. Strategically we permeated her hometown of Philadelphia and gave the Philly media complete access to breaking the campaign along with grassroots,

Black/urban media. The plan was for the grassroots movement to swell and create such excitement, passion and fervor that the mainstream media would reach out to get on the bandwagon. Within, 7 months of the project being released, record sales doubling each week, the calls were heavier than rain and I was selecting from *TIME*, *Newsweek*, *USA Today*, *LA Times*, *PEOPLE* and the list goes on and on.

RESET MOMENT *If you are getting rejection and believe in the product, then create your own movement and start using your mouth.*

Word of Mouth is Power : *By Mister Mann Frisby*

This is the deal.

If you're going into business, you need a decent marketing plan and a solid public relations strategy. This philosophy not only lends itself to major corporations and platinum selling recording artists. Even if you're selling tampons and pumpkin seeds out of the trunk of your car, this applies to you. Yes, tampons and pumpkin seeds!

If you have the saltiest, most absolutely delicious seeds this side of the Mississippi and no one knows they're for sale you're in trouble. If your tampons are of the highest quality and competitively priced, yet they're packed away in boxes in the trunk of your Honda, you can call it a day. But I digress.

My experience thankfully is in book, and not tampons. As a reporter for the *Philadelphia Daily News* I received countless press releases on a daily basis. I can say that most of them were stuffed in my wastebasket before I even finished my lunch. It was not that I did not have interest in covering a particular business or event, but timing was truly everything. Many times entrepreneurs and company executives alike, simply didn't give me enough time to put anything together.

For example, if you have a small, relatively unknown business, do not send out press release on Monday for an event you have planned for Saturday. Give editors sand reporters enough time to consider working you into their pages. Space is tight and you have to keep that in mind. I can't stress that enough. You are competing with dozens of others who want that same blurb in the Friday entertainment section.

I self published my first book, *Blinking Red Light*, in May 2002. I knew from the beginning that it was going to be a challenge simply because I was new to the industry and a relative no name. With that in mind I started pushing my book a few months prior to its release. I had small handbills printed up with a synopsis of the book on one side and the cover on the other. I knew that the audience for BRL would be primarily Black women, who devour good fiction, so I made it my business to be where Black women were. I handed them out at the mall, clubs, and conventions. I even did the 4 a.m. let out of a male exotic dance show because I heard that the promoters were expecting six hundred women. Bingo!

When I did my first signing on May 11, 2002, I sold one hundred books. Of those sales, sixty or more women said that they had one of the handbills already so that they've heard about my book from a friend. Depending on what your product or service is, don't put all of your energy into securing publicity in newspapers and magazines. Word of mouth goes a long way and is often times more effective. If you do choose to pursue print and broadcast media as your primary source of publicity keep these things in mind.

Press is press is press. Even if a local talk show is not interested in highlighting the unique qualities of your tampon collection, there may be another angle. I received plenty of rejections from media outlets after I pitched my new book. However, many of those same outlets agreed to give me ink on my status as a working single father or my accomplishments as a mentor and track & field coach to dozens of youth.

There is an old cliché in journalism that should hold true to your goals as an entrepreneur. When a dog bits a man that's not a story, but when that same man bites the dog back – now that's the story. Make sure your business or service equates to you getting on all fours and sinking your teeth into that dog!

Mister Mann Frisby (yes, it's his real name,) is a native of South Philadelphia, and a motivational speaker, track & field coach and author.

Notes

_____
_____
_____
_____
_____
_____
_____
_____
_____
_____
_____
_____
_____
_____
_____
_____
_____
_____
_____
_____
_____
_____
_____
_____

Notes

Notes

30 DAY RESET:
Brand, Business & Bottom Line

CHAPTER 9

Work It!
Leverage Your Contacts

IF THERE IS ONE IMPORTANT lesson I can pass along, is that networking is paramount and essential for any business to succeed.

Networking is key to grow your business, secure clients, and build lasting relationships. How effective you are in coming out of your shell and being your own cheerleader will determine if you win at this game. Understand the networking game ... have a clear vision of your objective, make lasting connection and impression, follow up, stay in touch, be prepared for the opportunity.

Networking, as an art form seems very intimidating; however, just think of it as socializing with your friends, but on a much larger scale, greater platform with higher stakes.

The following tips will help you stand-out at an event:

- Feel good about you. Smile and act like the winner you are
- Be prepared with your objective, write your notes down and review
- Practice in the mirror how you want to appear in front of people (watch for facial expression and body language)
- Have business cards on hand and give out 2 at a time in case they're misplaced
- Make it your business to meet at least (5) new persons each time you network
- If you attend with friends, separate. Groups are intimidating
- Listen and observe before you engage in a conversation
- Always look for a common thread when talking to someone for the first time
- Be sober and coherent

- Firm handshake and eye contact
- Brevity is best—get in, get out, state your mission
- Have fun, remember your objective

Networking : Lacey Clark!

Most people think that networking is about putting on your best suit, tie, shoes or heals, buttoning up your top button and having a firm handshake, but for me, networking is about being "you in (best) form" …shining from the inside out.

I call it the three B's of networking:

1. Be your most positive self

Being your most positive self is about authenticity. Personally, I like to find something positive about a person and highlight it, put the emphasis on that one thing that may shine. Every human being likes to feel good. I like to offer honest compliments that make a person feel good about being a human first beyond their title because, believe it or not, underneath the expensive suit and tie and/or heels is a person that more than likely has the same wants and desires as you. I love to smile. A smile is usually infectious and you would be surprised how something as simple as that can make someone's day.

2. Be Bold

Being bold has everything to do with thinking outside of the box, finding your personal strength and courage and presenting that unapologetically. No, I don't mean swinging from the chandeliers to make your grand entrance into a meeting. It is about the duality of being humble and confident at the same time. There are whole lots of people who are afraid of their greatness, even the ones in suits. The closer you get to your greatness the quicker people will respond to you. Remember, it's about being humble and confident at the same time…it's not about being better or worse that anyone else.

3. Be in the right place at the right time…every place is the right place.

Being in the right place at the right time is about knowing that every place is the right place. You never know in whose presence you are and how someone can further you on your path or how you can further another on her/his path. Now, I am not asking you to be overtly friendly with people in restrooms and strange places. I am simply stating that everyone deserves a smile, eye contact, and a kind word here and there. In fact, some of the most honest connections are those that are random and happen when you least expect it.

Basically, be you...beautifully, authentically, truthfully. Everyone can't be the coolest person in town, or a size six, or be trendy and hip. Believe me, when you are trying to be someone you are not, it shows. And, when you are comfortable in your own skin you can't hide it. So, when networking, remember that the uniform is secondary to "you in (best) form."

"You are shining star know matter who you are, shinning bright to see what you can truly be."

—Earth, Wind and Fire

Lacey Clark! is a life coach, founder of Sisters Sanctuary.

Notes

_____
_____
_____
_____
_____
_____
_____
_____
_____
_____
_____
_____
_____
_____
_____
_____
_____
_____
_____
_____
_____
_____
_____
_____
_____
_____
_____
_____

Notes

_____
_____
_____
_____
_____
_____
_____
_____
_____
_____
_____
_____
_____
_____
_____
_____
_____
_____
_____
_____
_____
_____
_____

notes

30 DAY RESET:
Brand, Business & Bottom Line

CHAPTER 10
Re-Invent Yourself

ONE MUST ALWAYS BE PREPARED to re-invent one's life, career, and place in the universe. Life is always changing, evolving, and you must flow in accordance. The person you were at 23 will not be the same person at 23, 33 or 43 for that matter.

Three years ago, I decided to resign from my post as Jill Scott's publicist. It wasn't because I disliked my job, the people, or the mission of the product. The fact of the matter, I was completely burned out and no longer had the desire to craft/design campaigns. It was better for me to leave my post on top, than have my poor attitude reflect the project. It was a challenging decision that I prayed on, consulted my husband, family, friends and prayed some more and some more. I knew that somewhere, deep inside me the woman, Karen Taylor Bass, was ready to shine and march to a different beat. I just didn't know that it would be challenging, difficult and depressing at times. When you have worked with someone for 7 years that is all that people know and think of you. I was known as Karen Scott, Jill Taylor, and, sometime my real name Karen Taylor (wasn't married for much of the duration of my tenure with Jill). I had become an extension of Jill and that is all people wanted to see.

I truly had to think about what it was that made me happy, what did I want in my (new) life, what did it look, taste, and feel like? How did I interact with people, what was my message? Did this vision incorporate my family, did it require traveling, how would I make money, did I have a 5-10 year plan? Truthfully ... it took me 3 years to figure out the plan, and believe it. While I was re-inventing myself, I relied on my inner circle to keep me together when moments of doubt would creep into my thoughts, paralyze me and my FICO score would plummet.

I believed, in my re-invention and started to put my plan into effect.

- I am a PR Expert, could masterfully consult and train individuals to utilize the media as a tool of empowerment
- Believe in my power, daily affirmations and journaling
- Write for various magazine, utilize the media to get my message out there
- Have clarity and know message like my home address
- Speak for free for practice, practice, practice
- Network, Network, Network
- Introducing myself to people, speak into existence my vision
- Tap into database, let people know what I am doing and ask for help
- Join professional organizations and let my agenda be known
- Create a newsletter to promote my company, vision and others
- Volunteer at events to give back to my community
- Creatively try to brand my company with events, merchandise, alliances ... **(most failed due to poor thought and execution)**
- Be smart and don't waste valuable time
- Do something different and get different results
- Partner with talented and super smart people
- Send out 1-2 press releases per month and inform people what you are doing
- Listen to your inner voice and ask God for guidance
- Don't be afraid to fall, fail, and be broke. It's all temporary
- Know and believe that you are a winner
- Align yourself with the best ... then you become the best
- Read and learn from those you respect
- Secure a mentor
- Trust in God and have patience

Re-Invention : Regina Robertson

Contrary to popular opinion, career transitions are not for the faint of heart. I, for one, have endured many detours along the way and have been guilty of questioning myself at every turn. I even have a few bumps and bruises as evidence of the challenging, yet rewarding, task of changing course.

Looking back, I can finally appreciate the abundant amount of opportunity afforded to me as well as the freedom provided to pursue an unorthodox path. As such, I've enjoyed a career of finding and thriving in all that has interested me ranging from fashion, music, film and the written word. What I've learned over time is that at each crossroad, I've had to buckle down and get focused on my goal before I could formulate a strategic plan of attack. Regardless of the direction in which my arrow is pointed, the following principles have assisted me in navigating the path to my target:

- ■ Understand the industry that you wish to be a part. Read the trades, surf the net and "Google" those whom you wish to learn more about.

- ■ Don't be afraid to reach out to people in your field. Some will be receptive while others might be lukewarm, but you'll never know unless you e-mail, fax or make a call.

- ■ Request an informational interview and start building your contacts.

- ■ Get out, mingle and meet people. Networking is one of the best ways to get your name and face out there.

- ■ Market yourself! Instead of relying on the typical means of promoting your talents, try taking it one step further (i.e. build a website).

- ■ Always send a handwritten thank-you note to those whom have taken the time to share their knowledge and contacts.

- ■ Most jobs can be learned. Take the time to build upon your skill set and be sure to leave room for learning more as you go.

- ■ Be patient, stay focused and remain persistent. You will get there.

Regina R. Robertson is a journalist residing in Los Angeles, living her bliss, and loving life. www.reginarobertson.com.

A Business Simply Can't Survive on Passion : *by Agnes Davis*

As a business owner approaching my 6th year at the helm of **swim swim swim I SAY**, I can honestly look back and say, WOW! What a ride! Wait a moment, how do I really mine that the good, bad, highs, lows, discover, pitfalls? ALL OF IT!

I first must let you know, I had entrepreneurs in my family my entire life. Growing up, I had no idea what an entrepreneur was or how it influenced me. All I knew was that my mom and dad worked very hard, and owned a food confession stand during the summer months when I was a kid. The most interesting part was they also had full time jobs. I just thought everyone's parents hustled like mine. I was a kid; what the heck did I know. The "work hustle" my parents showed me was my norm.

Following college and several different jobs later, I finally ended up in the medical field in a job that I loved. But one day in 2008 a week before Christmas, all of that glory I had put into my career was taken away. Almost one month later, I was wrongfully terminated from the job that I loved so much. The toxic environment that I had endured for over 5 years but for some reason did not want to escape, removed me very abruptly. To be honest, several people helped me escape but it was not on my terms. Looking back, there was a plan for me that I would have never guessed for my future. At the time, all I saw was fail-ure. How do I explain to the two most important people in my life, my parents, I got fired! Well, I did and as most of you already guessed, they were amazingly supportive. However, I quietly went into a depression with a smile on my face like everything was okay. I knew things had to change, but I had no clue how. Let me just add, I worked out /swam prior to losing my job and I continued throughout this period. This may seem like a very weird entry, but you will see as I explain (more) how it plays a very important role in where I am today.

In March of 2009, we saw the worst crash of the stock market second to the Great De-pression. As I lay on my couch and watched The Today Show soon after the crash, Donny Deutsch had a segment about starting your own business. I came out of my self- induced coma and started to listen. He stated, "Even though this is one of the worst times in our economy, this is the best time to start a business. I know people will think I'm crazy, but it is." He went on to say,

"Do something you love, make a niche and the rest will come!" It got me thinking, why not me; what am I good at and what can I do? At first I cried and thought I wasn't good at anything, but I stopped and thought deeper. I was a really good swimmer, with loads of experience, and thought maybe I could turn that into a business.

I started to think back to my days of learning how to swim and thought who were my teachers and what did they look like? Except for my mom and sibling, no one looked like me; why the hell not?! After placing that question in my mind, I figured let's start research-ing swimming lessons, learning how to swim, etc. Let me just say, the Internet revealed to me more than I understood, knew or bargained for. I quickly found out there were no swimming company owners who looked like me, who serviced Upper Manhattan/The Bronx exclusively. I dove deeper and the one theme that kept popping up was child-drowning rates, especially among minorities were highlighted in most listings. I guess because I knew how to swim, swam on a team and had no fear of water, all of this made very little sense to me or should I say, this phenomenon was not my experience. But the statistics about drowning especially minority drownings, and how people had no access to a pool or were so afraid of the water, intrigued me. I knew in my heart of hearts, I could make a difference.

Little did I know, but right at that moment, my business was born, **swim swim swim I SAY**. In my mind I wanted to start a swimming company that would cater to the residents of Upper Manhattan/The Bronx that offered quality-swimming lessons by a diverse staff. But, I felt strongly that because of my knowledge and experience as swimmer, I needed to be on the frontline taking action to decrease drowning rates for all, but especially minorities. This was just the beginning of my journey.

I compiled all of my research, statistics, facts and started swim swim swim I SAY's busi-ness plan. For most, the business plan is a very tedious visual document but necessary tool to gather your thoughts, ideas and give your business direction. I learned quickly what certification was recommended and liability insurance needed. Pool facilities were not cheap to rent and pool rentals were few and far between in Upper Manhattan/The Bronx. I also looked at competitors in the market to see what they were and were not doing. I knew I needed to be different and better.

To keep from going crazy since I was terminated from my full time employment, I ran and swam even if snow was on the ground. I entered one of the few NYC owned recreation facilities that had a pool one morning and a post seeking Water Safety Instructors for the summer. I contacted the City of New York and was told, I had to take a WSI course and become certified. I immediately acquired the $450 certification, paid another $250 for my lifeguarding certification, and began to teach swimming lessons during the summer to kids through a free program. I was on my way!

This job was a mental barometer to reinforce how good of an instructor I was. It proved to me that I could do this and do it better than what I was experiencing. Imagine, I was the newest instructor at this pool in Upper Manhattan and, by the second summer session, parents were pissed I was not teaching their child. The parents saw what I already knew about myself that I was really good! What did the summer of 2009 give me? Time and space to test my knowledge on what I already knew while quietly building my business. I also learned very quickly that fear of water students were welcome in the summer programs but there was no formal class or handbook on how to teach these students.

I met a very bright and amazing instructor, who, like myself, was not a 16-year-old kid looking for a summer job. We became very close and I told him of my plans (this new friend would end up working with me down the road). I truly believe, at times, you must go to a competitor, not speak of your idea and see what the real deal is from the inside. You may think this is sneaky, but let me give you a clue; most successful people who have an idea, test it out somewhere else (first) and become successful after seeing what can be done better on their own. Research a new, but powerful vodka brand and see who is laughing all the way to the bank while others were laughing at him. BRAVO!!

While teaching for the City of New York, I started the next phase of my business. I was very fortunate to meet a gentleman back in 1997 who was a banker. I stayed in touch with him over the years as he moved up the corporate ladder, moved to different branches and became a bank manager at a different bank. Little do we know, when we meet people, form a business relationship and **NOT** burn a bridge, how monumental that person can be in our journey? With that being said, who do you think I went to for advise about starting my business and money; the moneyman himself. He gave me free advice and great direction to really open the doors of my dream. He informed me I needed to incorporate to open a business account, look at marketing, advertising, putting together a website and start looking at how I was going to acquire clients. I returned to the bank quickly with my corporation papers in hand, an EIN number, and a check to open the account. Now, the big question, where did I get the money? I was working only part time teaching swimming, living off my savings because my employer denied my unemployment, got black listed in my medical profession, still had a mortgage to pay and car payments. What the hell was I thinking but I used some of my savings to open my business account. The funds for mar-keting, advertising and renting a pool in the Upper Manhattan/The Bronx area also came from my savings account. Basically, I just jumped off the cliff and hell, I forgot the para-chute!

It was time again to move to the next phase of my plan — a website, advertising and marketing. The banker recommended a young man doing websites in my area. I gave him ideas of what I wanted it to look like and after several meetings and drafts, I had my very first website. I thought it was great and amazing! As I just said, I thought it was great and amazing. At the same time, I did business cards, 4x6 printed cards, searched for clients and learned where to advertise to attract clients. I basically walked the streets and started placing the stock cards anywhere that was kid friendly and would accept them. I went into a kid business, **The Little Gym**, and spoke with the owners. They welcomed me with open arms and even asked me to give a lecture to their parents on swimming. Lets just say, no one showed up, but our relationship was great. I found a pool to rent in the area, purchased a $3,000,000 liability policy and continued to peddle my cards, which started get-ting inquiries. **swim swim swim I SAY** got its first three clients in October of 2009! As I taught these students, I took out a full-page advertisement in one of the popular parents/children magazines and landed three more students!

I was now running a business from the inception to the delivery of the product. Remember I mentioned an instructor I met back in the summer? Well, I still spoke with him regularly and saw him, from time to time, at the city pools. He got a lead from a friend that a school with a pool in Harlem, NY needed a swimming instructor to teach their entire student body. He suggested and I agreed we do it as a team. I set up a meeting with the principal, asked what her needs were and how she felt we, Clay and I, could help the schools achieve their swimming goals. Following the meeting, I met with a businessman I was dating at the time and asked him to help me put together this proposal. I researched the In-ternet, let him add his knowledge and presented to the principal/school a full plan on how 2 instructors were going to teach First through Fifth Grade (at least 150 kids) swimming. **swim swim swim I SAY** got the job.

We presented the school with all of our documentation, certifications, insurance policies, and registered forms with the city as a business doing business with a school and had waivers for the student's parents to sign. This was great for the company and great for us. But immediately as we started to teach, we encountered many fear of water students. Clay and I knew we had to come up with ideas ourselves because there were no manuals on how to fix this problem or guides to help us. In addition, we started to see fear of water clients at our private location more often than we imagined. We talked extensively on the fear of water situation and knew WE had to write some type of manual. So from what others would not tackle or face, **swim swim swim I SAY** wrote, copyrighted and trademarked the *FIRST Fear of Water to Loving the Water Swimming Curriculum*. Our niche was officially documented!

As I look back on my company and where we are now, I can truly say I don't think I made tons of mistakes but boy, one big one was coming down the pipeline. Imagine, in all the excitement of landing the school contract to teach at least 150 students, I forgot to find out how **swim swim swim I SAY** would get paid by the City of New York. **HUGE MISTAKE! Don't make this mistake!** Find out how you get PAID, always! I had the signed contract, money was agreed upon, it was sealed, and delivered but no money after 2 weeks of teaching. Following a visit to the principal's office, a very nice secretary informed me I needed to submit invoices to the school, have them scanned to an office downtown with our attendance records and then the invoice would be paid. OMG! Neither Clay nor I saw a dime for 6 weeks. Due to my relationship with Clay, he hung in, but that could have been a huge disaster.

I also learned, as my business grew, my worth became more apparent to myself and how no one could place a price on my value. Why do I mention this? I feel people try to change or tell you your worth. I have two comments concerning this: **1.** Don't allow anyone to dictate your worth, and **2.** You better be able to back it up! I'll never forget the day a parent called me for lessons and wanted to come, but felt my prices were too high. She literally said, "I will give you this amount and you should take it." I told her "NO", that is not the price and she said when you don't have enough students you can call me back and we can work it out. That was 5 years ago and I never called her back. It was confusing to me how some-one wanted me to take less for my skills, but I'm sure if someone had asked her to take less for her skills, she would be very angry! The bottom line—**KNOW YOUR WORTH** and **DON'T FORGET IT**.

Clay and I continued to work as a team and discuss many things. I have to say, Clay kept me reaching for more because he believed in my dream and saw my passion and determination. **swim swim swim I SAY** continued to advertise to help with our expansion, but the money spent was not doing what I needed for it to do. I knew I had to separate myself from the competition. We started to put more focus on the Fear of Water swimming classes and expanded our client base by offering lessons to tots children and adults. I started attending community meetings; spoke at schools, on the bus, subways, in the grocery store and even in the store where I purchased my hair products. I knew I had to expand my audience by different means so out of my comfort zone I went.

I went to my hair product store and chatted as usual with a salesperson who I had met several times before. She knew I had a swimming business and we would just catch up as I shopped and talk about swimming and how to take care of all types of hair. This one day she told me about a free class she was taking at the **Harlem Business Alliance** on social media, branding and the Internet. I missed the first two classes but she said there was a great instructor, she was amazing and I really should attend. Now let me tell you, I knew nothing about social media. I hated Facebook, and the Internet was for looking up things and branding was something done to animals on a farm! But she insisted I should attend and learn all about branding, social media and the Internet to expand my business. So out of my comfort zone I went again and attended the next class. Deep down inside I knew that branding was the new buzzword. The Internet had a power all to itself and social me-dia in conjunction with the other two had become the biggest avenues to be an ultimate game changer for any business.

The night I attended the seminar and it changed my business forever. I met the amazing Karen Taylor Bass. She addressed pitching, branding, social media and how all of these aspects affect your business and how you are viewed. I took notes and participated willingly. I have to admit, the class was great and I learned so much. Karen even offered at the end of class to take a quick look at your website and she would provide brief feedback at the beginning of the next class. I was so excited to hand her my business card so I could get some positive feed back. The next week rolled around and I asked her if she took a look at mine. She very politely said it was "ok." I was floored but my saving grace that night was I presented a good pitch to the group. With one week left, I knew I had to absorb as much as possible and I did. Karen showed how social media of different magnitudes could drive your business and change the entire dynamics of how you are viewed and your product received. As the last class wrapped up, Karen offered an amazing deal to have a one on one with her and she would present to you what changes she thought would be helpful to drive your business. The cost was unheard of to me, an expert was reviewing your dream and the information she would provide would be invaluable. A PR expert re-viewing the website and business giving you honest feedback was a NO BRAINER!

I contacted Karen, a week later and she forwarded a questionnaire that was so thorough, you had to explain the smallest details of your business. I won't lie; I was a little overwhelmed so I put the questionnaire to the side. But leave it to Karen, she checked in to say she had not received the questionnaire back and asked if was I overwhelmed. I admitted I was, but I promised her I would get through it soon and I did.

The entire process plus the upcoming face-to-face meeting was the best thing I could have ever done for my business. Karen reviewed my website, business cards and my competitors and had four pages of notes to review at this meeting. Karen asked right at the start of the meeting what I did for a living besides the swimming company and after I replied she said now it makes sense. I asked her to explain and very clearly without any hesitation she said, "Your website is STERILE!" In my head I was like damn, no she didn't. She did not stop there. She proceeded to explain why it was sterile and explained to me what my competitors had done to make their sites fun. Karen explained to me that swimming is thought to be fun and my website had no fun. Karen wasn't looking for me to be like my competitors but to evoke an emotion not sterility! I was able to ask questions and learn about social media and how it could change my business while she guided me in a diction better suited for my business type. I left that meeting NOT defeated but empo-ered to set forth her changes.

Soon after that meeting, I attended a meet and greet of my neighbors/business owners in the complex where I reside. A gentleman, his wife and I starting talking. I noticed he was a photographer and a web designer. He offered free of charge to look at my website and give me some feed back. I handed him a card and waited for his reply. After a few days, Bruce and I talked. He was so pleasant but he said the one dreaded word, "Sterile," that made my hair stand up! I was shocked, not because he replied "sterile" but because Bruce and Karen had never met and said the exact same thing. Bruce also added that the colors I chose meant the kids were on fire! The truth had been spoken. I felt at that moment I had found another person that could help grow my brand and business with a competitive website. Both Karen and Bruce became my confidants and advisors for my company's new phase. Team **swim swim swim I SAY** was officially formed and together we were going to change the outcome of the game!

As **swim swim swim I SAY** grew, the milestones came with it. Most may think the biggest accomplishments for my company would be the development, growth, amazing media coverage and longevity; however, none of the above could compare to what happened in the pool with a fear of water client. Imagine watching a swimming student go from crying to just put their foot into the water to swimming 4 different strokes. The best word is PRICELESS! To know that you studied, wrote, thought about different ways to get this student to just put their face in the water let alone swim, speaks volumes! That is so rare to be witness to a moment of joy that cannot be duplicated. That achievement is worth more to me than any amount of money because now one more child is safe from drowning and **swim swim swim I SAY** made that difference!

As I started this story, I looked back on my last 5 years and explained to you how I am approaching my 6th year. I am happy, proud and blessed by what has come my way. It has taken an excellent PR expert, Karen Taylor Bass aka KTB, believing in my vision, helping me expand my vision, hard work, good listening skills and great customer service to be where I am today. What makes my company different than most is the way I conduct business. I want every single client to walk into the pool area and feel like it is one big family. Good morning and their name or a big "hi" will always greet them. As a consumer and a business owner, I feel most businesses lacking good customer service and pride in the delivery of their services. Imagine, I was good to go in my medical career and it was gone in a blink of an eye. Even though I fought the system, got my job back at the same facility, watched those involved move on, I had to hit RESET even though I had no idea, that was what I was doing. Looking back, RESET meant changing my mindset, being a business owner and having a passion for something other than myself. I was never a selfish person, but now I could give back by letting others know "your life in the water matters."

Agnes C. Davis, CEO, swim swim swim I SAY (sssIS), the only female minority-owned and operated swimming company in New York City. ***www.swimswimswimisay.com.***

Notes

_____
_____
_____
_____
_____
_____
_____
_____
_____
_____
_____
_____
_____
_____
_____
_____
_____
_____
_____
_____
_____
_____
_____
_____
_____
_____
_____

Notes

_____
_____
_____
_____
_____
_____
_____
_____
_____
_____
_____
_____
_____
_____
_____
_____
_____
_____
_____
_____
_____
_____
_____
_____

Notes

_____
_____
_____
_____
_____
_____
_____
_____
_____
_____
_____
_____
_____
_____
_____
_____
_____
_____
_____
_____
_____
_____
_____
_____
_____
_____
_____
_____

30 DAY RESET:
Brand, Business & Bottom Line

CHAPTER 11
Mentoring

I HAVE BEEN MENTORED THROUGHOUT my life. Some of my mentors have come from watching television, (Oprah Winfrey) to my grandmother. Mentors come in all shape, size, ethnicity, some I know (personally), others I admire from a far. The bottom-line is that mentoring is imperative for growth, development, and evolution.

When selecting a meaningful mentor, understand the reason why you want one. A meaningful mentor is a person that will be responsible and receptive to you ... your ideas, time, energy and passion. Don't get fooled by someone that is good on paper and irresponsible in person.

RESET MOMENT

When securing a mentor, make certain that you don't select someone solely based on his or her executive title and positioning. Make a selection based upon thought, research, references and commitment to you.

Mentors (also) have to be accountable to you, and you to them. Do your research, interview your mentor, and ask the questions listed below.

1. *Will you be able to commit to mentoring for 1 year?*
2. *May we touch base once a month via telephone, email? Set up face time 4 times a year?*
3. *May I attend a professional meeting with you to view you in action?*
4. *Do you volunteer, if so, may I accompany you?*
5. *How can I be of assistance to you and your goals?*

Make mentoring meaningful, realistic and have fun. It's reciprocity and being accountable to each other so that everyone WINS. Most importantly, you must mentor someone yourself to give back to the universe.

KEEPING YOUR MENTOR ACCOUNTABLE

Role of the Mentor: The mentor will provide individualized support, assistance and guidance to a newcomer or an individual changing positions within a chosen profession/field.

Mentor Requirements:
- Is considered by peers to be knowledgeable in the field.
- Sets high standards for self.
- Enjoys and is enthusiastic about his/her field.
- Continues to update his/her knowledge in the field.
- Is committed to be a mentor for at least one year.
- Letter of recommendation from Mentor's boss indicating that the potential mentor is qualified to serve as a mentor and that the company will support the program.
- Available via email and teleconference 3x a month (minimum)

Successful Mentor Traits:
- Listens and communicates effectively with others and is able to provide constructive feedback.
- Recognizes excellence in others and encourages it.
- Commits to supporting and interacting with colleagues.
- Recognizes the needs of others and knows when to offer support, direct assistance or independence.
- Exercises good judgment in decisions concerning oneself and the welfare of others.
- Admits mistakes and learns from them.

(*taken from the Mentor Handbook, 2000*)

Notes

Notes

Notes

_____
_____
_____
_____
_____
_____
_____
_____
_____
_____
_____
_____
_____
_____
_____
_____
_____
_____
_____
_____
_____
_____
_____
_____
_____
_____

30 DAY RESET:

Brand, Business & Bottom Line

CHAPTER 12
Honor Thy Process

TRULY HONOR YOUR PROCESS. The process is how you feel through the highs and lows as you position yourself for the best opportunity. It's not going to be easy, but I promise you if you stay focus and surround yourself with positive loving people, trust in a higher being you will make it and succeed.

The words Honor Your Process is truly the best gift I can share with you. Take time for yourself; be silent as you figure it all out. Allow God to manifest within you, talk to you and visualize your glory. When you go against the laws of the universe all types of crazy things begin to happen and you have to reboot and start all over. Don't waste time, listen to the inner voice and honor your process.

I always knew I was talented, working as a Media Strategist allowed me to actualize and realize my gifts to create, implement and pitch winning campaigns for all genres. The challenge however, was seeing a greater vision for myself, not allowing others to define me by their limitations. I de-

RESET MOMENT *Live your life with purpose and enjoy God's blessings and vision for you.*

served so much more and it wasn't until my 37th birthday that I decided to honor my process and make real changes in my life. Knowing I wanted to make changes was not easy, it took me an additional 2 years to take the first step.

At 39, during my pregnancy, I saw myself grow and become a better person, little by little I learned how to humble myself, trust my instinct, and start to blossom. Upon turning 40, all bets were off, I was determined to make my dream come through ... become the ultimate PR Expert, motivational speaker, author, radio host, and consultant. I started to treat my company as if I was on retainer, created a press plan, wrote press releases, pitched myself to the media, and stayed focus despite rejections.

My modus operandi is to succeed globally, prosper, and build a brand to compete with the best while simultaneously empowering individuals. Honoring my process one day at a time.

When a Boss Chick Stops being the Boss : *by Karen Taylor Bass*

Lets get something out of the way - I am not the poster child for postpartum. I am a boss chick! I'm about big moves, creating media campaigns and taking celebrities and making them a brand. I relished my role as the strategist; it was I that Stevie Wonder called when he needed a crisis handled; it was I who wrote the groundbreaking campaign for an unknown D'Angelo, 18 years ago which introduced the masses to *'Brown Sugar'*; and, lets not forget the international media campaign for *Who's Jill Scott*? I am that chick and had it all handled.

I was career focused; every move was a chess game and did not see the postpartum malaise coming. At the tender age of 35, I decided it was time to get married and created a campaign to find a husband. Got married at 38 and started to prepare my body for a baby, and gave birth at 40. Life was on my side until it knocked me on my ass.

This story is not just about postpartum depression; it's about life, being 40, losing your way, and fighting to get back to self. Ultimately, it is about pressing reset with your brand, business and bottom-line. Trust me—they are all one in the same.

Seven months into my pregnancy, my life took an unexpected turn. What happened next changed me and kept me imprisoned for 4 years. Being diagnosed with Placenta Previa, then bed rest for the remainder of my pregnancy, a complicated delivery; and, internal clotting which resulted in doctors manually pulling clots out my vagina coupled with 2 blood transfusions. The process left me mentally and emotionally exhausted and I snapped. I was under 24-hour watch after the transfusion and the doctors weren't certain I would make it. God saved me, however, I stopped living. I managed to breastfeed my daughter for 17 months and gave her everything I had, but gave self nothing. Absolutely nothing.

 I went from loving life to not leaving the house. In fact, it took me several months to get out of bed and check the mail. I stopped having sex with my husband; what was supposed to be a year off, which multiplied to 4 years; credit score plummeted; and the anxiety and depression kept mounting. Often times, I wondered if the anonymous blood from the transfusion was taking over by body and I was taking over 'that' personality. Sounds crazy, right? My husband told me six months after the birth of our daughter that I needed help. I asked him if he thought I was suicidal. He said he didn't know, but I was different. He gave me the number of a support group for post-partum and a number for a group called **Mocha Moms** (support group for women of color); I put the information down and went back to existing.

When you have postpartum depression and don't treat it, it starts to take over your body, mind, and soul. Not only am I depressed, can't leave the house, now I'm having acid reflux and panic attacks. I mean full-blown panic attacks where I'm rushed to the emergency room and treated immediately. The cycle became repetitious: enter the emergency room with a crazy blood pressure like 180/120. The doctor would order a battery of tests, have me relax, then take my blood pressure 30 minutes later and it would be 109/75. The doctors asked me about my mental state and prescribed an acid reflux drug. My husband said he wasn't leaving work early (again) to come to the ER and not to call the next time. I was crushed, but understood.

One day while breastfeeding my daughter, I took a really good look at her and wondered if my unhealthy mental state would impact her later with behavioral issues. At that moment, I started to cry, I mean a come to Jesus cry. How could I have been so selfish and fucked up? I love my baby and fought to have her, is this how I show it? That was the day I took a baby step to heal. I decided to start with the basics - taking a shower, combing hair, opening the door to check the mail and (eventually) graduating to walking around the block. I started going to therapy and went searching for that number for **Mocha Moms**.

I also started journal writing, working out and discovered yoga. Yoga saved me. I started to feel better after each class and was inspired to stage a comeback. After all, this is what I knew best.

Getting a job was a real challenge, especially since the economy sucked and I had no experience in social media. I had to reinvent, learn new skills and brand self as the PR Expert; got a non-paying part-time gig for experience as a blogger for *Black Enterprise* and started writing a book, *You Want Caviar But Have Money for Chitlins: A Smart Do-It-Yourself Guide for those on a Budget* which is now a best-seller on Amazon.

I work each day now on staying strong mentally and physically. The acid reflux and panic attacks have been MIA for three years and although I have moments from time to time, God is not done with me. As the PR Expert, this boss chick is no longer the go-to celebrity publicist. She is the ultimate PR Expert for small businesses, entrepreneurs, executives and savvy individuals. Most importantly, I am the woman that has pressed RESET.

Here's to your RESET!

Karen :)

30 DAY RESET:

Brand, Business & Bottom Line

Congratulations

YOU ARE READY TO GROW your business.

Email me at *Karen@karentaylorbass.com* and tell what steps you have completed to publicize your product.

If you are interested in having Karen Taylor Bass, *The PR Expert*, speak to your organization, school or group, contact me through my website **www.karentaylorbass.com.**

Stay in touch, sign up for newsletter and continued progress.

Karentaylorbass.com
Taylormademediapr.com
TheBrandNewMommy.com

30 DAY RESET:
Brand, Business & Bottom Line

Recommended Reading

Becoming A Category of One
by Joe Calloway

The Purpose Driven Life
by Rick Warren

The Money Coach's Guide to Your First Million
by Lynnette Khalfani Cox

Say It With Power and Confidence
by Patrick Collins

Communicating Effectively for Dummies
by Marty Brounstein

Consulting for Dummies
by Bob Nelson & Peter Economy

Succeeding Against the Odds
by John H. Johnson

Who Moved My Cheese?
by Spencer Johnson, MD

The Personal Touch
by Terrie Williams

The E-Myth
by Michael E. Gerber

Elements of Style
Strunk and White (a book on grammar and writing)

Any good dictionary

The Holy Bible

30 DAY RESET:
Brand, Business & Bottom Line

About The Author

Karen Taylor Bass
The PR Expert
www.karentaylorbass.com

KAREN TAYLOR BASS is gifted. For almost three decades she has taken a solid approach to creating unique media campaigns, taking under-performing or unknown brands from obscurity to notoriety.

Karen has created strategic public relations, branding, and marketing campaigns for corporations, luxury brands, celebrities, athletes, and entrepreneurs. Her talent is crafting engaging media campaigns while simultaneously securing media placements. Karen's placements range from the Associated Press, ABC News, *Washington Post*, *USA Today*, Yahoo News, Oprah, *New York Times*, AOL Parenting to *Entrepreneur* magazine.

Bass started out as a fundraiser working for the United Negro College Fund and United Way of NYC, to raise funds for various charities represented by the United Way. Bass exceeded her target fundraising goal by 30% within the first year and started to hone her skills as a communicator, writer and presenter to tap into her passion as a media expert.

Always up for a juicy challenge, Karen left the world of fundraising and embarked on a career in entertainment. A lover of music, she learned from her bosses at Double XXposure, EMI, Sony Music, and Time-Warner on how to write and execute award-winning campaigns to empower and engage consumers. Karen created memorable campaigns from Rap, Jazz, Neo Soul, Pop, R&B and Latin. Artists directly impacted by Karen's gift includes but not limited to: Arrested Development, GangStarr, Dianne Reeves, Boy George, D'Angelo, Jill Scott, Massive Attack, Mariah Carey and Proyecto Uno. The National Basketball Association (NBA) representatives tapped Bass to create campaigns for Chris Webber and future hall of famer, Ray Allen.

That's not to say Karen's accomplishments haven't come without any bumps in the road. Following the birth of her youngest child, Karen suffered from post partum depression, lost her confidence and took a three-year hiatus from public relations. Bass understands what it is to press reset and change the course of one's path by embracing setbacks. "I've been through a lot mentally, spiritually and professionally upon giving birth to my daughter at the tender age of 40. With that said, I bring determination and courage to each campaign, project and client I work with because I now understand the power of pressing reset for one's brand."

Bass has been featured as a PR Expert and 'Brand' Mom in several media outlets including: Dr. Oz, CNN, BET, NBC Today, Fox-TV, ABC-TV Here and Now, WPIX-11, *Entrepreneur*, *Essence*, *Newsday*, *NY Daily News* and more.

Bass has authored a best-selling book (peaked at #18, Amazon) on public relations and branding.

Named *Top 20 PR and Brand Expert to follow @ Twitter at ereleases.com.*

Order Books by Karen Taylor Bass

IF YOU'D LIKE MORE information on products offered by Karen Taylor Bass, please see the website at **www.KarenTaylorBass.com**.

The following books/ebooks can be found on the website:

You Want Caviar But Have Money For Chitlins: A Smart Do-It-Yourself PR Guide for Those on A Budget (Top 20 bestseller on Amazon)

The 'Brand' New Mommy: From Babies To Branding To Bliss (learn how to renew your life) Foreword by Jill Scott

TaylorMade Books are available at quantity discounts with bulk purchase for educational, business, or promotional use. For additional information, please contact, *info@taylormademediapr.com.*

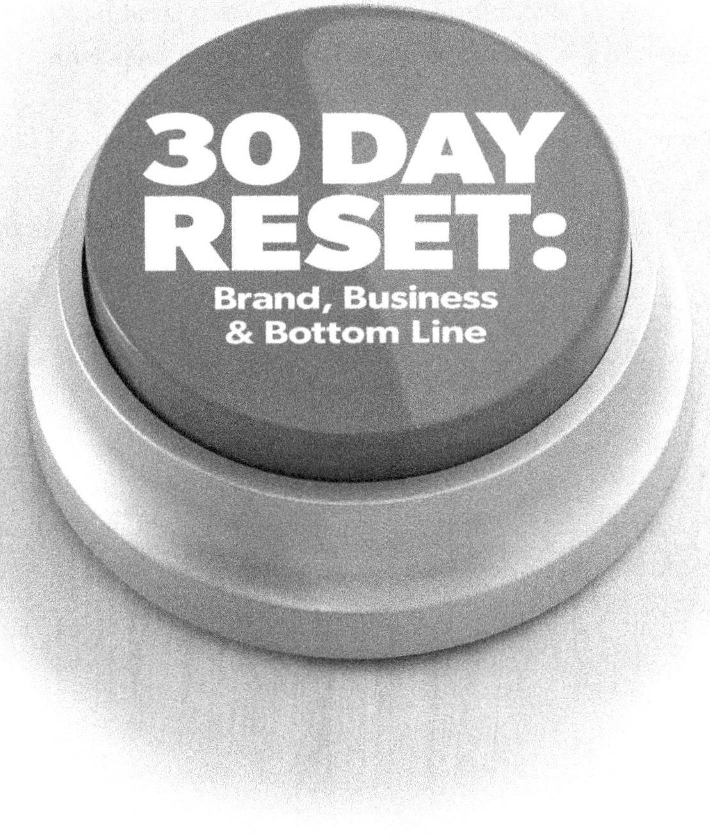
30 DAY
RESET:
Brand, Business
& Bottom Line

www.ingramcontent.com/pod-product-compliance
Lightning Source LLC
Chambersburg PA
CBHW032322210326

41519CB00058B/5360